I0483946

Photography for Beginners:
Your Complete Beginners Guide to Mastering Digital Photography & Taking the BEST Photos

Copyright 2014 by Brendon Ward - All rights reserved.

This document is geared towards providing exact and reliable information in regards to the topic and issue covered. The publication is sold with the idea that the publisher is not required to render accounting, officially permitted, or otherwise, qualified services. If advice is necessary, legal or professional, a practiced individual in the profession should be ordered.

- From a Declaration of Principles which was accepted and approved equally by a Committee of the American Bar Association and a Committee of Publishers and Associations.

In no way is it legal to reproduce, duplicate, or transmit any part of this document in either electronic means or in printed format. Recording of this publication is strictly prohibited and any storage of this document is not allowed unless with written permission from the publisher. All rights reserved.

The information provided herein is stated to be truthful and consistent, in that any liability, in terms of inattention or otherwise, by any usage or abuse of any policies, processes, or directions contained within is the solitary and utter responsibility of the recipient reader. Under no circumstances will any legal responsibility or blame be held against the publisher for any reparation, damages, or monetary loss due to the information herein, either directly or indirectly.

Respective authors own all copyrights not held by the publisher.

The information herein is offered for informational purposes solely, and is universal as so. The presentation of the information is without contract or any type of guarantee assurance.

The trademarks that are used are without any consent, and the publication of the trademark is without permission or backing by the trademark owner. All trademarks and brands within this book are for clarifying purposes only and are the owned by the owners themselves, not affiliated with this document.

Contents

Introduction 1

What is Digital Photography? 3

    Non SLRs 6

    SLRs 6

DSLR: What is it? 10

The Basics 11

Shooting modes...14

    Shutter Priority (TV or S) 14

    Aperture Priority (Av or A)................................15

    Program (P) 16

    Manual (M) 17

    ISO...17

    Metering 19

    Exposure Compensation......................................21

Focusing 23

    Automatic Focus modes of DSLRs 23

    AF-C..23

    AF-S 23

    Focus points..24

Image manipulation...26

    Rules of third..26

    Manipulate your image using zoom lens and focal points 28

Making your image pop 29

Use the flash to your advantage 30

Framing Your Photos 32

How to Stop Taking Boring Photos 35

Conclusion...39

Bonus Content!..40

Introduction

Are you thinking of buying a digital camera and are wondering why you should buy one and not the other? Do you know the quality of photos that each camera type can produce? Are you wondering why your photos are not as amazing as that of your friend Dick despite him using a lesser powerful camera? Is he using some magic? Do you feel as if there is something wrong with your digital camera or even DSLR camera just because you cannot seem to take excellent photos, as you would have wanted? Do you feel that your photos do not tell the story the way you would have wanted to tell it? This book will help you to transform from a beginner digital photographer who is always complaining about how they cannot take a good photo to a pro photographer who takes the most creative photos in the most bizarre places.

What is Digital Photography?

Before I can explain what digital photography is, perhaps I should clear some confusion between digital imaging and digital photography. In a nutshell, digital imaging refers to the art and science of making and manipulating digital photos, which are usually represented as bitmaps (in this case, the work could be done using a digital photo using a camera, through scanning a photograph or through capturing frame from video). On the other hand, digital photography involves the use of cameras that contain rays of electronic photo detectors that capture images that are focused by a lens (this is a replacement to films).

After creating the photo or image, you can opt to add some special effects using different image enhancing software after which you can then print the photo using a photographic paper or a normal printer. In simple terms, it is the kind of photography whereby an image is exposed, captured and then stored digitally and not on film. One outstanding feature of digital photography is that you can produce instant photos, which are of low resolution.

Just as there are different sizes of camera film, digital image sensors come in different sizes. In essence, smaller sensors capture lower quality photos compared to larger sensors. For instance, cell phone cameras, and smaller point and shoot cameras usually have lower quality images compared to DSLR cameras. So, how do you stand to benefit when you are using digital cameras?

1. You get to review images instantly-this means that you can adjust whatever you want instantly so that you can take better quality photos.
2. Digital cameras cut costs tremendously-you don't have to buy film every other day since you will be saving photos on a memory card. If you don't want some photos, you can delete them to even free up space.
3. You can view images on TV, computer or even print them using a normal printer. This makes them very convenient.
4. You can have a lot of information about the photo including date, the location the photo was taken and lots of other information. This can really help you to remember important moments in your life.

5. With digital cameras, you can change ISO, aperture, and shutter speed, in order to capture better quality photos. In digital cameras, you can change these settings from picture to picture unlike in film cameras whose ISO is dependent on film in use, which cannot be changed from one image to the next in one film.

Well, I know that you know most of these benefits; that's why you would probably not even think of acquiring a film camera.

So, what makes the difference between a superb digital camera and one that is not so good? The answer is pretty simple; the sensors differ! Sensors have different pixels (this is the number of photo-electronic conductors that are in an image sensor). Given that every sensor has millions of pixels, describing it at megapixels is a better description for the camera resolution. In essence, if you hold all things equal, a camera with a high resolution captures better quality photos.

Let's first understand the different types of digital cameras available before moving on to how you can use digital cameras to take better quality photos.

In a nutshell, there are two broad types of digital cameras based on the nature of lenses they use i.e. the non SLR and SRL digital cameras.

Non SLRs

With a non SLR, the lens is fixed onto the camera (it is not interchangeable). These are also known as Point and shoot digital cameras and don't usually allow you the photographer to see whatever the lens is seeing i.e. its viewfinder doesn't look through the lens.

Cameras that fall into this category include your camera phone, point and shoot (compact digital) cameras and bridge compact digital cameras or simply super zoom cameras.

SLRs

The SLRs allow you to remove the lens from the camera (mount or unmount) and their viewfinder looks through the lens, which basically means that you see what the lens is focusing on. These include the digital SLRs and the Mirrorless Interchangeable Lens Cameras or Compact System Cameras.

I will not go into too much detail about the types of digital cameras that are available; instead, I will concentrate more on teaching you about how to take the best photos using digital cameras. In a nutshell, if you are using anything none SLR, it will mostly come with automatic features except for the super zoom or bridge compact digital cameras (these allow manual aperture priority, shutter priority, aperture priority, program mode and semi automatic modes-it also has a higher zoom), which means that they give you more control over how to take photos.

Nonetheless, if your goal is to simply take decent, sharp photos, which don't require much thought or action on your part besides just powering on the camera, pointing at the subject and then pressing the shutter button, you really don't need an advanced camera since the modern point to shoot cameras are pretty enough for that job.

Actually, all you need to do is to combine your quality image with some very basic photography composition principles and you will have more than what you need at a fraction of what you can do with a DSLR. Well, DSLRs are powerful, but costly, a bit complex to understand and are often bulky (you can't fit them in the pocket!). With that said, you would wonder why you actually need a DSLR as opposed to just using the non SLRs cameras at your disposal. The reason is pretty simple; with DSLRs, you can capture, sharper crispier photos (you need high quality and often costly lenses to do that). DSLRs can also handle some challenging light conditions including night photography, and sunsets thanks to their greater flexibility features that make it a lot easier to capture the photos that you are looking for.

As you can probably notice, I wouldn't be teaching you how to capture photos using a camera that doesn't give you any flexibility (something that only operates on auto mode!) because you really don't need to do much to capture good photos with these cameras (well, they cannot even get to the quality of a DSLR captured photo). The purpose of this book is to help you compose/capture excellent quality photos while you have some freedom to manipulate the photo by changing camera settings (not just zooming) such as operating on manual, shutter priority mode, aperture priority mode, and other modes. This book will also teach you some basic photo composition tips that work across all digital cameras so that you can capture photos that tell everything you want to pass across.

So, when is a DSLR going to really stand out from all the other cameras? Well, you might probably not notice any difference in the quality of photos when you view them on a computer monitor. However, if you intend to print large pictures, a DSLR will produce the photos with all unmatched sharpness.

Since achieving excellence with DSLRs calls for patience, learning and hard work, you might probably find yourself taking worse of photos than point and shoot cameras if you don't know how to use it properly and like a pro. As such, experimentation really comes in handy.

As you can note from direction the book is taking, you will need to get a DSLR if you want to capture the best photos. Let's narrow this discussion to DSLRs before I can mention how to manipulate photos using any digital camera (some features will work better on DSLRs).

DSLR: What is it?

Digital single-lens reflex (DSLR) cameras seem to be growing in popularity lately. Do you want to know why? Because you can manipulate such features like aperture, ISO and shutter speed. In this book, I will teach you how to work with the exposure triangle (ISO, aperture, shutter speed) and other DSLR features to your advantage. I will also teach you how to compose excellent photos using the right focus, framing and angle positions, image manipulation tips and tricks and how to make the most of the lens just to mention a few things. If you are looking forward to sharpening your digital photography skills, then you are reading the right script. Many people after getting intimidated by the manuals that come with their DSLR cameras simply unpack it and start shooting photos. The result is that they never really get the best of their DSLR. So if you are a beginner who is unsure of how to make the most out of their digital cameras, this is a perfect starting guide.

The Basics

As earlier mentioned, many people easily feel intimidated by the large manuals that come with their DSLR cameras. This might be because of limited time or simply because they are tired of the perceived jargons that are used in the manual. They consider the easy route, which is unpacking the camera and starting shooting; in any case, they know how to press the shutter button! Well, you have to realize that you have a DSLR and not a point and shoot camera if you have been following this route! While this will work for some people, many fail to reap the most out of their digital cameras. This section will help you understand some of the basic features of a DSLR so that you know what each does and when you should use it. I don't intend to replace your manual in this section; I will simply help you to understand it with greater ease. To start from the very beginning, I will first give you a scientific understanding of what a DSLR camera is; I will not assume you really know what you have.

DSLR camera

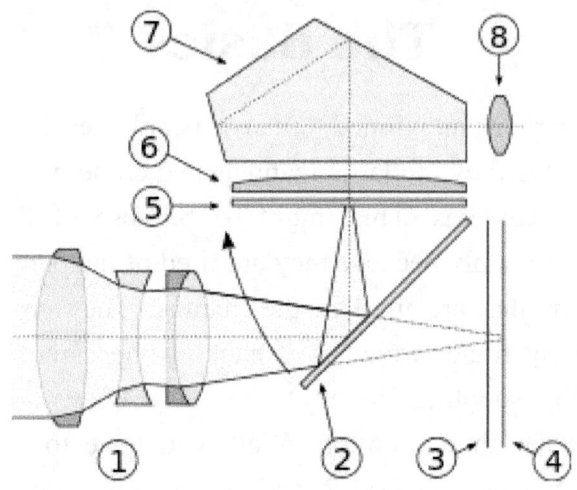

Key

1. Camera lens

2. Reflex mirror

3. Focal-plane shutter

4. Image sensor

5. Matte focusing screen

6. Condenser lens

7. Pentamirror or pentaprism

8. Viewfinder eyepiece

A digital single-lens reflex camera is a camera combining both optics and mechanism of a single-lens digital camera combined with a digital image sensor instead of a photographic film. The above figure is a perfect demonstration of what really a DSLR camera is.

The DSLR camera differs from other cameras in the way the reflex design scheme is composed. With the reflex design, light travels through the lens through a mirror, which in turn alternates to pass the image to the viewfinder or image sensor. With DSLR, the viewfinder has its own lens hence the name single lens. This gives the DSLR advantage over other cameras in that the viewfinder presents an image that is exactly the same as the one captured by the camera sensor. Please ensure that you understand the above figure as we will use it later on in this guide.

Before you start shooting, let me explain the different shooting modes that your DSLR will probably allow.

Shooting modes

The best place to start our discussion is on shooting modes. The shooting modes include 'auto', AV, TV, P, M' and many others depending on the manufacturer. It is good to know that different manufacturers abbreviate the shooting modes differently. For instance, yours could be abbreviated as A', S', P, M' or anything. Nonetheless, they all function in the same manner. The shooting is important since the shooting mode that you pick will determine how your camera behaves when shooting photos. If for instance you pick auto as shooting mode, then your camera will automatically select everything within the exposure triangle i.e. shutter speed, aperture and ISO automatically.

Shutter Priority (TV or S)

This is a semi-automatic shooting mode. It is mostly abbreviated as TV or S depending on the manufacturer. In this case, you will have to set the shutter speed and the camera takes care of the aperture as opposed to aperture priority (discussed below). The shutter speed is the amount of time the shutter will stay open when taking a photo. This time is mostly measured in seconds or more often fractions of seconds. The more time the shutter stays open when capturing a photo, the more the amount of light that will enter the sensor. So, what is in the shutter speed?

You would select a faster shutter speed if you are capturing a fast moving object like a flying bird. If you are capturing a moving object that is blurred for example a waterfall, you should use a slow shutter speed if you want the photo to come out blurry. A slower shutter speed will require that you place your camera on a tripod so that it is not interfered with in the process of capturing the photos.

The good thing with this mode is that you don't have to worry about everything; as you take care of the right shutter speed, the camera takes care of the right aperture and ISO.

Aperture Priority (Av or A)

Aperture is the size of the opening in the lens of your camera through which light is allowed to pass through anytime the shutter is opened for shooting. The amount of light passing through this opening depends on the size of this opening. The smaller the aperture, the lesser the amount of light will pass through it.

The aperture of your camera is displayed as a ratio of the focal length to the diameter of the aperture or opening. It is represented by an f-number e.g. f/2.0. , f/2.8, f/4.0; a larger aperture has a lower f-number.

Choosing the right aperture is one of the most crucial things about photography. It directly influences the depth of the field i.e. the amount of an image that is in focus. If you pick on a larger f-number i.e. a small aperture, then it would mean that a large distance within the capture scene is in focus.

Small f-number (a large aperture) will achieve a shallow depth most appropriate when you are interested in a photo whereby only the subject is in sharp focus while the background remains soft and out of focus. So next time you are using your camera, you should try to manipulate the depth of your field and get complete control of your camera.

Program (P)

This mode provides a meeting point between the semi-automatic modes of aperture or shutter priorities and manual control. In this mode, you will set either the shutter speed or aperture and your camera adjusts the other one accordingly. If you change your shutter speed, the camera automatically adjusts your aperture and vice versa. This sound so easy, doesn't it? You only have to master how to set up your aperture priority or shutter speed and the other will automatically adjust.

Manual (M)

This is exactly manual. You have the full control over everything such that you can set both your shutter speed and aperture. There will be an exposure indicator just below your screen or viewfinder that shows you how your image will look like. Determination of the correct exposure is however left to you.

Understanding how the various shooting modes affect the quality and orientation of your photos is a perfect point when it comes to learning how the combination of aperture and shutter speed settings affect your photos. You can only get better at it through practice.

ISO

This measures the sensitivity of the sensor of your camera to light. Even though this term was coined during the era of film photography where films of different sensitivities were used in different shooting modes, this too applies to digital photography.

It is numerically represented from ISO 100 (low sensitivity) to ISO 6400, which denotes high sensitivity (this could be higher depending on how powerful your camera is). The ISO is quite important as it controls the amount of light that is required for adequate exposure.

Where do you I use low ISO numbers?

As I already told you, low ISO numbers means low sensitivity. This is particularly useful when taking photos in the sun. This is because there is a lot of light hitting the sensor and therefore the sensor does not require to be more light sensitive. It means that if you are using your camera in the sun, then you should use a low ISO such as ISO 100 or at most 200. This will result in quality photos.

And what about high ISO numbers?

This works when there is a low concentration of light in the scene where the shooting is taking place e.g. when taking photos in a dark or poorly lit room. At such conditions, there is not as much light hitting your camera sensor and therefore the sensor must be highly sensitive. In this case, you will set up a high ISO number such as 3200 to increase the sensitivity of the sensor. A small amount of light is therefore multiplied to give you the correct exposure. However, this has an effect of interfering with the quality of your images by introducing what looks like fine grains on the surface of your photos.

Generally, you should keep your ISO as low as it is possible. The lower the ISO number, the higher the quality of your images given that they will have no grain. In the sun, an ISO of 200 is good for your camera. It will save you much trouble if you know what ISO figure works where. For example, if you are shooting photos on a sunny day, you can start with an ISO of 200 to see how it fares. If indoors, you can pick an ISO of about 1600 and use it as your starting point.

The good news is that most digital SLRs have an auto-ISO installed where the camera automatically sets the ISO depending on the amount of light in the environment. This auto-ISO tries to keep the amount of light as low as it is possible. Do not ignore this feature of your camera though; it is what keeps grain or noise at minimum.

Note:

Understanding the relationship between the shutter speed, aperture and the ISO of your camera adds up towards producing better quality photos. These three make up what is commonly referred to as the exposure triangle.

Metering

In our previous discussion, I have maintained that when using the ISO, shutter speed or aperture priority or automatic modes, your DSLR camera will always calculate the exposure based on the amount of available light. The camera will try to establish an average exposure by assessing the entire scene or field, both the dark and bright areas, and come up with an image that is averagely 18% grey. This is called metering.

Metering is the reason why when you shoot an object in poorly-lit room, it likely appears brighter than it actually is. It is the same reason why an object, which is much brighter will appear darker than it actually is. The camera will probably average the scene to make your photo correctly exposed.

Your digital camera has modes that allow you to take control of your camera by controlling the areas of the field you would like metered. These modes are:

- **Average:** This mode will meter your image to 18% grey; this is also known as middle grey after assessment.

- **Centre-weighted:** The camera will weigh the exposure reading of the field through the viewfinder and ignores the extreme corners of the image. It covers approximately 80% of the total image field.

- **Stop metering:** This concentrates on a small area of the scene say 55% of the viewfinder area. It assesses the dark or light conditions in this small area and exposes the entire field to middle grey from the assessment.

Note: It is always advisable to start with either average or center-weighted metering mode if you are a beginner. Pick one mode and stick to it. It will enable you to understand when a particular scene is over exposed or under exposed when you compare it with how you see it with bare eyes.

Exposure Compensation

I mentioned that whichever metering mode you choose, you should be able to know whether your photo is under or over exposed. So, what happens in case it is under/over exposed? Let's discuss that.

Exposure compensation function is usually on a small +/- button found near the shutter. It gives you the freedom to increase or decrease the camera's default meter reading mode to reflect the actual level of brightness.

If say, a field that contains bright tones is produced as too dark by the average meter mode, you can use the positive exposure compensation to produce a scene that is much brighter. The opposite will call for the use of negative exposure compensation.

The above basics summarize what is contained in your manual. Learning these basics is a good starting point to gaining control of your camera and I hope you can now understand what comes to play when it comes to excellent photo shooting. In the next chapter, we will discuss about focusing. How do you produce a photo with the right focus? Let's discuss all that in the next chapter.

Focusing

While shooting modes allow you to get the right exposure for your image, your image will surprisingly be different from what you wanted if you do not get the right focus for your subject. You must get the right focus for you to produce the best photo. But just how do you focus your camera correctly? This chapter is designed to solve this puzzle.

Automatic Focus modes of DSLRs

Nearly all DSLR cameras come with autofocus modes. These modes however vary from manufacturer to manufacturer in attempt to beat or secure their market segment. I will take through two, which to me are the most important modes.

AF-C

Autofocus-continuous is used when shooting moving or action subjects. It is achieved by half-pressing the shutter. Focus is acquired and then locked to the subject. The good thing is that even as the subject to be photographed moves, the focus will also adjust with it and this continues until the photograph is taken.

AF-S

Autofocus-single is used when shooting subjects that are stationed at certain points. For example, you can use the mode when shooting people, structures, portraits, or buildings. It is also achieved by half pressing the shutter, which brings into focus the subject and locks the focus on that point until you long press the shutter button.

It is important you note that autofocus modes will only work when you turn on AF i.e. autofocus on the lens. You should not confuse the MF-manual focus or AF- autofocus with the above discussion. Those are completely different functions.

Focus points

The autofocus modes we have discussed in the above sections rely on focus points. A look through your viewfinder should enable you to see many squares or what looks like dots across the screen. Whenever you half-press the shutter, one will be highlighted in red. The highlighted dot is the focus point and it is its position within the frame that the camera will focus on.

Most people make mistakes by leaving their cameras on full autofocus mode with the belief that their camera is going to choose the best focus point for them. This is not appropriate as only you know what to focus on. There can be no better option than you choosing your own focus point.

The best way to do it is to ensure that you initially set up your camera to a single focus point. This way, you will be able to choose whatever you are focusing on so that you can ensure that your subject is always on focus. After several repetitions and practice, you should probably be in a better position to change the focus point without having to take your eyes off the viewfinder since this is likely to distort your image when you move.

Image manipulation

Did you know that you can employ the features in your camera to influence picture sharpening, coloring and contrast when you are shooting in the above discussed shooting modes? Well, that is what you can do with your new DSLR camera. In this section, we focus on tips and tricks that can help you achieve this. Your camera is fitted with picture control features that can be manipulated to give you your wildest image you have ever thought of. I will display to you this in the following tips:

Rules of third

Use the rule of thirds to capture amazing photos. With this rule, you can tell whatever story you want to tell.

Rule of thirds at work

Have you noticed that your camera has an option for displaying grid? When you display this grid on your horizontal screen, it is broken down into 9 even squares, right? In this case, you have three horizontal and three vertical spaces, which allow you to place your image at whatever position you would like. You can put your picture in the top, bottom, left or the third right of the screen but the middle place is no placement zone.

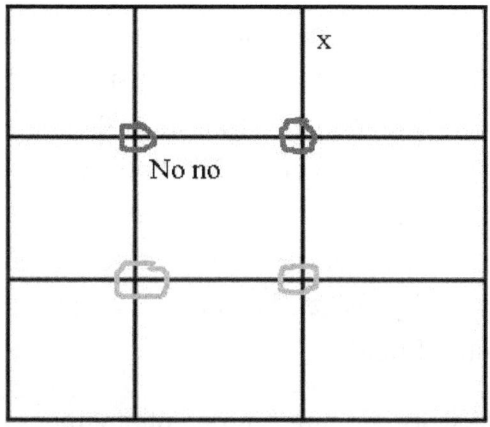

The idea of making the middle a no no placement zone is that you want to split the image into 1:2 ratio (one third and two thirds) and not to half it. This is what is called the rule of thirds.

This rule makes your photos to appear static as opposed to when you place them in the middle. If you place your picture in the middle, you limit the extent to which the eye can view your art. Place it near the edges say x and let the eye follow it. This makes your art more interactive and the idea can stay longer on your image.

If you look keenly in the above picture, you will notice the intersections of the line on the grid. Those intersections are called focal points. Keep it in mind we will refer to it later.

Sometimes it may be necessary to break this rule. You only break a rule if you understand it. Breaking rules when it comes to art produce the best creative works but only if you know how to successfully break or bend them. In photography, if you are looking for balance, then it is justified to place your image centrally. When bending this rule please note your depth of field.

This rule works in any kind of photography whether you are using a DSLR camera or not. So, don't be shy to use it even when using a point and shoot camera.

Manipulate your image using zoom lens and focal points

A zoom lens is any lens that magnifies a part of the image and makes it appear as a full image. That is exactly what your DSLR camera can do to you. Well, other cameras can do that but you need to get closer to the subject for this to work well. The zooms lens magnifies the images by changing the focal points. The further the focal point is away from the image sensor inside the camera, the more magnified the image will be. Different lenses have different zooming powers so you have to choose one that is ideal for the kind of photography you want to undertake.

For instance, lenses with a focal range of above 100mm are called telephoto. These allow you to zoom in action. The high zooming capability makes it ideal in animal photography given that you might not really get close enough with a point and shoot camera! That crazy moment that your friend won't simply pose for the camera will be captured from your hide out! You can also alter your focal point to isolate your subject from a crowd.

Making your image pop

Your camera allows you to alter the color of images as much as you wish. Additionally, you can control the amount of light that goes through the lens in order to make your images pop.

Since we had discussed about the aperture previously, we will only give a brief statement on how the aperture affects the quality of your pictures. The main point here is to know that controlling the amount of light makes them either sharp or blunt. When it comes to color change, your camera has options through which you can control the contrast or background. When shooting in the P, S, A and M exposure modes with your DSLR camera, you can tweak image sharpness, color and contrast.

Use the flash to your advantage

Most beginners don't understand when to use flash and when not to. This is especially so when shooting during the day. However, you will be amazed to discover that your digital camera's flash feature is a lot more than just a tool for notifying the subject that a photo has been taken! So, how do you use it to manipulate your images.

Use it indoors and use flash in poorly lit areas (it doesn't have to be at night!). However, if you want your story to be that the photo was taken at night or in a dim environment, a flash won't be necessary; instead, you can work around this by adjusting (increasing) the ISO. If you want to use flash in an area with white ceilings, which are not too high, simply mount the flash on your DSLR then bounce light off the ceiling or any white walls in the surrounding. Well, don't try to bounce flash in any other color since light has a tendency of assuming the color it was bounced from (you can bounce on a different color if that is what you want to achieve). All you need is a bounce card or a piece of white paper; you mount this on top of your flash. You could even capture through an umbrella.

You can also use flash in combination with adjusting exposure compensation up and down especially if you are shooting in backlight. This should produce photos where the subject is well exposed.

Framing Your Photos

Framing can be better understood as a deliberate act to block other parts in the scene so that the viewer's attention is drawn to the object of focus. We often do framing as a way of displaying and calling attention to our most favorite sections of shots. While many disregard framing as an exercise in futility, there are many benefits of framing your images. These include:

- It gives your images a sense of depth. It adds something in the foreground hence adding an extra dimension to your images.

- Frames lead the viewer to your most critical focal point. Frames provide the barrier between your photos and other barriers. In this way, it is able to keep the eye longer on the subject.

- Framing has also been used to give photos context. If for instance, you are shooting animals in a park, you use a frame that reflects the context of these photos hence communicating something extra about the environment. In simple terms, it helps tell a story.

- Frames also hide other things present in the scene. Psychologically, there are people who are drawn to your images simply because they would like to know what is hidden within the frames. Frames can therefore intrigue your viewers.

Even with the above advantages that come with framing your photos, getting it wrong when framing can be disgusting to the viewer. It might not tell the story you want to pass across making the viewer confused on what exactly you wanted to communicate in your photo. It is therefore necessary that you get it right if you are to achieve you desired goals.

Photographic frames come in various shapes and sizes. It can include shooting through Windows, doors, overhanging branches, tunnels, arches etc.

Framing your photos need not be stressful if you know what to consider when framing your pictures. So, what is it that you shouldn't overlook when framing your photos?

What to exclude from the frame: To direct attention to your subject, then you should be able to know what is to be blurred and what to make conspicuous. If there are trees in the background, then the framing should be in such a way that they do not become the most attractive part of the image if they are not the subject.

Ask yourself what the frame will achieve. Will it add or take away from the image. Sometimes the frame can be the difference between an ordinary shot and a stunning shot.

Framing if properly applied can give flavor to your pictures. However, framing must be done with care and professionalism as a bad frame can water down an otherwise good image.

How to Stop Taking Boring Photos

They say a picture is worth a thousand words. In the previous chapters, we concentrated in helping you take control of your camera. In this section we remind you of some of the obvious but often forgotten tips in taking images that are attractive and not boring. These points may seem obvious to most people but many often get them wrong:

- Make sure your lens and sensor is clean before going into a shooting spree. Ensure you use a cloth specifically designed for this purpose. For sensors, simply blow over it even though most digital SLR automatically clean the sensors. This is a pretty easy exercise and should not be the source of dirty photos for you.

- Get your subject in the right spot. Make sure your subjects are correctly positioned where you would want them to be. If you are interested in featuring the background, then make sure you do so without interfering with the subject.

- Do not forget to read your manual. It sounds boring, but it is for a good course. The book is not meant to water down the use of that manual. Different manufacturers produce different features. It is important that you read your manual to identify how your Nikon camera differs with a different model.

- Framing your photos is very important. Nonetheless, remember that too much framing has an effect of making your images clumsy or cluttered. Refer to our previous chapter to get the best of it.

- Do not ignore the effect of lighting in your work. Lighting sets the mood and atmosphere for your photos. In cases where you are using external lighting, make sure the correct level is available. Be sure to use sunlight to your advantage. For internal flash, ensure you understand how to use them. I already discussed this in the image manipulation tips section.

- Control the exposure. You have shutter speed, aperture, and ISO among other features under your control. Use them to your advantage. Being able to control this exposure manually is the best for you. Automatic modes work in general cases but are not where you want to pay special attention to something in your image.

- Always have your camera ready. Photos are meant to capture moments. Unfortunately, moments only last for a moment. Keeping your camera in a locked safe is never a good idea. A friend once told me he missed an opportunity of a lifetime. His sister-in-law had spotted a snake and shouted out of fear. He rushed to his house to get his camera to capture the reptile but when he came back, his brother had already smashed its head. He therefore missed an opportunity of shooting the snake alive. Do not be caught up in the same scene. Be on the alert.

- Understanding about the depth of your field and how exposure affects the size of what is in focus will boost your creativity greatly. Learning about the effect of shutter speeds, aperture size, and other shooting modes will give your work a great boost. This is why I always emphasize that you should learn the manual operation of your camera. The more you learn how to use your camera's manual mode, the better you can get at it because you can use everything to your advantage.

- When capturing portraits, it is advisable that you shoot vertically. Vertical shooting really suits certain shots and you should not be afraid to try it out.

- Learn from others. It is as simple as that. Be sure to compare with others and be keen to notice points of differences; what you like and what you don't like. Embrace objective criticism while doing this.

- Experiment: Don't just limit yourself to taking photos in the modes or settings I mentioned. The great thing with digital cameras is that you don't have to worry about using up the film since you can always delete photos that you think are not necessary or those that you don't like. You also have the freedom to reset the camera settings when you feel as if you have messed up all the settings. The more you experiment with different settings, the more you will learn.

Conclusion

I hope you enjoyed this book. If you are starting in photography, I recommend that you reread this book as there are many tips and tricks mentioned that will assist you in turning your ordinary digital photos into professional masterpieces.

In summary, the book starts by introducing you to digital SLR cameras. It then brings to your attention some of the most important aspects of DSLR photography including focusing, framing, image manipulation and many more. I hope you have learnt something you didn't previously know about digital photography.

Bonus Content!

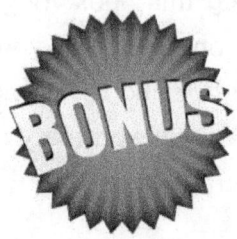

As a token of our appreciation <u>Grand Reveur Publications</u> would like to give you access to our exclusive bonus content (including free eBooks!). <u>You're only a click away from receiving:</u>

Exclusive pre-release access to our latest eBooks
Free Grand Reveur eBooks during promotional periods
A method ANYONE can use to publish their own book and make passive income

https://ignorelimits.leadpages.net/grandreveurpublications/

As this is a limited time offer it would be a shame to miss out, I recommend grabbing these bonuses before reading on.

www.ingramcontent.com/pod-product-compliance
Lightning Source LLC
Chambersburg PA
CBHW071011180526
45168CB00003B/1383